T0147742

BREAKFAST
with
my
FATHERS

Kevin M Isaac

authorHOUSE®

AuthorHouse™ LLC
1663 Liberty Drive
Bloomington, IN 47403
www.authorhouse.com
Phone: 1-800-839-8640

© 2014 Kevin M Isaac. All rights reserved.

No part of this book may be reproduced, stored in a retrieval system, or
transmitted by any means without the written permission of the author.

Published by AuthorHouse 06/30/2014

ISBN: 978-1-4969-2074-4 (sc)
ISBN: 978-1-4969-2073-7 (e)

Library of Congress Control Number: 2014911053

Any people depicted in stock imagery provided by Thinkstock are models,
and such images are being used for illustrative purposes only.
Certain stock imagery © Thinkstock.

This book is printed on acid-free paper.

Because of the dynamic nature of the Internet, any web addresses or links contained in
this book may have changed since publication and may no longer be valid. The views
expressed in this work are solely those of the author and do not necessarily reflect the
views of the publisher, and the publisher hereby disclaims any responsibility for them.

DEDICATION

I dedicate 'Breakfast with my Fathers' to all parents doing their best to raise children amidst the competing demands of contemporary life, its many challenges and persistent self-doubts and second-guessing.

You are not alone. And like you, I live in hope that the things I do and say today will eventually make a real and positive difference in the lives of my children.

To my wife, Prangtip and our three enterprising and energetic musketeers, Preston, Kaden and Keira; I thank you for teaching me life every single day and for reminding me that life is still by far the best place to live.

I extend a special word of thanks to Uncle Stanley (Stanley J. Ciaputa) for his friendship, timeless wisdom, persistent encouragement and irrepressible good humor.

In memory of Mr. G. Dennis Isaac and Khun Manit Silpaarcha

Acknowledgement

I have been blessed three times with the gift of fatherhood. I am fascinated by the way it continues to inform and transform me. In many ways, it is making me a better person. A couple years ago, I received a text from an old colleague, which read, "Happy Father's Day to one of the few men who understand the true meaning of fatherhood."

As much as I cherish those words for their power and nourishing encouragement; I want to draw attention to those fathers toiling day after day, night in and night out to provide for their children; those who work selflessly to bequeath their children a future much brighter, more rewarding and enriched with greater promise than they themselves experienced as children. I salute and thank you.

'**Breakfast with my Fathers**' is quite similar in style to its predecessors; however, I hope that it better encapsulates my photographic voice in words. This collection holds a particular fondness for me; simply because as I journeyed back though the fields and back-roads of my mind; I was afforded a seat at this old table of life and allowed to feast on delicious timeworn memories—still fresh enough to fill me up. Also, it gave me an opportunity to recover several matured bricks, strewn across the grass fields of my mind, and to stack them neatly together finally. In making this journey, I have been able to build this wonderful house which slowly became a refuge and an ode at the same time.

I thank my Fathers and all fathers whose commitment, sacrifice and energy may never get the recognition richly deserved. In more ways than one, this collection is a tribute to fathers and to their sacrifice. And to them—the fathers who, for whatever reason, have been denied or by their actions have denied themselves the daily joys of fatherhood, I hope that through these some of these poems you are able to share this special gift.

To my friends who continuously inspire me to capture, what I hope are, their precise words and phrases; who share their experiences and time to provide me the grist on which to build suitable metaphors, images and stories, ideas and emotions; I say thank you.

And to my dear friend and brother, John, who all too suddenly and quietly kissed the breath of God; I say thank you for the memories.

To David, whose pen's deep insights and innate intelligence allow him to raid, dissect, appreciate and explain the intricacies of my poetic ruminations, I am indebted to you. Thank you for your contribution to this collection!

Dr Kevin M. Isaac ©

Preface

For Kevin Isaac "If hearts could talk, mine would whisper melodies out load" and in this volume we have those whispered melodies, lyrically expressed in verdant hews. For him, "Poetry… is the lens of the poet's soul…where wishes go to be reborn" and in this deeply personal collection old wishes are revisited while new experiences provide rebirth. It is a volume that speaks to life's journeys as much as it does to its stages in a collection of intimate reflections on what it is to be a son and father in all its various forms. It contrasts and compares very different experiences over a life lived in many places, both socially and geographically. The poet reflects on what it is to be the son of the Caribbean, and the father of his own destiny which has taken him far from its warming shores. Nothing is held back in this volume, and we are transported between his childhood amongst the sugar cane and white beaches of his Caribbean youth to the cosmopolitan landscape of his professional life from London to Rome.

Yet, we also are treated to his innermost thoughts; to the intimacy of his love for his young children, to the laments for the loss of his own family in St Kitts. In "Hunger Pains" he whets the reader's appetite for "coconut dumplings, breadfruit" and "dasheen" as a means to illustrate why "This heart feels unsettled by nostalgia" for a lost past. The volume's title, "**Breakfast with My Fathers**" lays out several themes of the volume. Not only is it a celebration of fatherhood, through reflections on his own childhood, his relationships with his father and father-in-law and experience of being "Dadda" but it is also a vehicle for a voyage through time. The breakfasts are a metaphor for beginnings, for youth, hope, expectations and these themes are explored in bucolic language through pristine memory.

They are also contrasted with notions of night time reflections of how time has elapsed and how wisely the intervening period has been spent. It is a collection that explores closeness and distance. It transports the reader back to a home and hearth "of pre-dawn rambles along sugar cane paths", to a time of parental security, simplicity and innocence and laments the distance travelled from that life and love. It contrasts the integrity of a small community insulated from the world by its common values and shining seas to the path that the poet now treads where high politics seems to inspire low cunning. Throughout the volume there is the nagging question, "whether you would approve of the path/ Life is choosing for me". Although asked of his late parents, it is a question which is mainly being asking of the poet himself. Yet, as well as exploring distance the author celebrates the intimacy and joys that love, family and fatherhood have brought. It cherishes the sublime pleasures of new parenthood in a way that every reader can identify with either through experience or anticipation. Its language is heartfelt and almost too intimate. Some poems read more like letters to his children's future selves and therefore we feel privileged to have shared them. Many are odes to love in its many varied forms; the love of fathers, sons and daughters, but also of hope, humanity and humility.

This volume's incantatory and lyrical poetry also expresses an abiding sense of values and vision that challenges much of modern-day life. His international range of interests and images enable him to expose the emptiness of so much that is taken for granted today. His work articulates a call for the return of innocence in the age of Auschwitz and Rwanda. His poetry expresses a clear commitment to the politics of freedom in the face of injustice. He captures truisms sharply, seeing for example, wealth rising on "the spines of poverty."

His poetry expresses a political vision of great compassion. He quietly punctures false empathy- "sponsor a child far away/anywhere but here." A sustained theme is the need for the respecting of difference, between people and generations. This is underpinned by a series of poems showing the depth and naturalness of faith. He explores the parallels that lie within society and draws out similarities that lie within them. He shows that the similarities that are within each of us too. The principles that underpin his worldview, and are expressed in a series of moving poems about his children, are credited to his parents. His work explores the duties and difficulties that parenthood and adulthood bring. He invokes his parents but the root of life for him is his children with their "melodies of smiles."

KEVIN M ISAAC

He sees that the challenge for parents is to nurture them, to "grow into characters" and he explores this movingly. The imagery of his poetry is shaped by a strong sense of the richness of the natural world. For him "Mount Nevis" is paradise. His children are his Eden. Isaac is a poet of hope, principle and laments lost innocence.

"Breakfast with my Fathers" explores a varied landscape of themes gifted to us from the pen of a globetrotting diplomat. He shines his intellect on hypocrisy and injustice at both a domestic and international level and offers his reflections on his private retreats from that world. His own career has in many ways fathered this inspiring volume. Paradoxically however, in order to represent, promote and protect the interests of his island paradise, this son of the Caribbean has been separated from it through his diplomatic role. Yet this very separation is responsible for these poems and the window on the human experience that they so warmly provide.

Professor David Hastings Dunn,
University of Birmingham

Table of Contents

And I miss their laughter . . .

I lie awake listening to them sleep
And I miss their laughter

I recalled their tantrum-ignited feet
Infectious demand for attention
And viral chants to get what they want
Extinguished only by this slumber

And I miss their laughter.

In the still restful darkness
I reminisce on the daytime
When they raced to the kitchen
Dragging me behind them
Shouting the brand new moniker "daddy"
As though they invented it
And owned the copyrights

And I missed their laughter.

I think of them scratching the furniture
Inscribing their manifestations on the white walls
Proclaiming rights to everything in sight
Making nerves fray and patience thin

And still I miss their laughter.

I peeked attentively into the aging darkness
And felt their love
I touched their gentle breath to keep them close
And prayed for morning to come sooner
That they wake
And remind me again
Why each night
I miss their laughter.

Take me back . . .

To innocence
To long days soaked with cleansing rains
And the gleaming air
Harboured flavours of multi-coloured chards of sunlight
Seeping down slowly from cheery skies

Take me back
To long light-hearted walks toughened with gaiety
And to the crisp tastes of minty green fields and fruit-choked trees
Where life embraced me and I returned the embraced
And I was without fear

Take me back
To tropical blue oceans
With waves racing and raging to shore
To play on dark stones and white sand
Like a grand piano
Accompanied by orchestras of pelicans and seagulls
in harmony

Take me back to soothing nights of innocent sleep
With unlocked doors
Unafraid to welcome spontaneous strangers as friends

Take me back to before
Before Auschwitz,
Srebrenica
And Rwanda were symbols of our merciless inhumanity

Take me back to a time when
Houses of God were hallowed sanctuaries
Before churches were abandoned by their shepherds
Scorched, defiled . . .
Coerced into surrendering the keys
And turn their backs

Take me back . . . well before civilised nations bickered,
Dithered in public
And under cover of daylight
Surgically extracted
Only
Their citizens

Take me back
To before men and boys were scientifically mined from homes
Encamped
Their stomachs emptied
Over nauseating spectacles
Of loud dreams dying slow, painful deaths
While television screen grew dizzy from callous images
Of hunger and pain
And Innocence watched
Its flames snuffed out

Take me back
To the days
Before cruel numbers tattooed into the epidermis of life
Was substituted for people's identity
And humanity repeatedly dehumanised itself

Take me back to innocence
before
Security fences
Became proper guarantors of peace and longevity
Well before
Human bombs
Unmanned aerial devices
Missiles of fear and distrust
Kept peace among enemies
Rather than build friendship

Take me back
To when only the elements fell from the skies
Only birds, insects and curious eyes darted like bullets
Shooting across neighbourhoods

Take me back
To innocence
When gossip was the cruellest weapon
Stockpiled in idle houses and corridors of power
Where busy-bodies did so much harm
Soldiers and guns were unnecessary

Take me back
To a time when neighbours helped neighbours
And communities of one tended the sick
Housed and fed the defenceless.

Take me back to Sunday school,
Morning prayers and school assemblies
When the Word of God
Stood for more
Than a violation of somebody's human rights to choose
And brought reassurance
That faith could move mountains

Take me back
To Innocence
To times of genuine handshakes that bind
When politics produced statesmen
Who changed the World
And politicians built nations
Not portfolios

Take me back
To when children honoured parents
And parents protected their children
From exploitation online
Behind closed doors
In callous parlours

Take me back, please
Even if
Only for the holidays

Feasts of life

Restless dogs howl at the dawn
Nervous cats seduce the light
Vendors rise early to tame wild berries
While anxious feet comb the grey streets
For morning treasures

His eyes tickled open by daybreak
Joined pre-dawn processions
Scanning neighborhoods
For fresh delights

Patangko with condensed milk
Spicy grilled pancake chicken
Roasted over open fire
Bathed in sauces and
Served with soy milk and cornucopias of fruits

His voice always tiptoed up the stairs
Ahead of his eager fingers
Eventually
They brushed against the bedroom door
To announce
Kevin, Sawasdee krup; maa kin kaow, krup!

Some days
Spontaneous quick drives along busy highways
Carefully claiming two lanes
Landed us in the quiet asylum of deep massages
Lasting hours
Punctuated only by a raspy voice
Sabaidee mai, Kevin?
Jep mai, krup?

Conversations were rich with questions
About life—the future—
Travel plans
Journeys across country
Stops to savor shades of delicious tastes
Rooted in the Provinces
Where friends and acquaintances were received warmly
Embraced with smiles

Nakorn Sawan, Supan Buri, Chiang Mai, Roi Et
Nakorn Pathom, Ratchaburi, Kanchanaburi, Phitchit,
Breakfast
Served fresh with juices of welcome
Plans over easy
Stares gently scrambled
To discern answers buried in my eyes
Probing questions
Descending strategically into the depth of intentions
About life
About plans of the heart
About perceptions
All simple questions
Urging me to prepare
For feasts of life
And breakfast with my fathers

Parallels

Words
Carved into sacred pages
Elevated on pulpits
Codified into natural law
Crafted into hymns
And set to music

Words written in verse
Sealed in commandments
Transformed into life
Lessons to define character
Thoughts, behaviors and personality
In parallels

Words
Just Words
Often in parables
Enshrined in stories
Recited in changing forms
Through gateways leading to differences
Contrasted against agendas
Indefinite and mysterious

I seek
To know difference
To understand
Dissimilarities developed from similarities
In the word

Just Words
Set to a life in evolution
Unable to distinguish
Rapture
Resurrection
Reincarnation
Prayer from recital
Blind faith from spirituality
Hunger for redemption
From temporal transcendence

Words
Quite similar
But seen not in Parallels
To be embraced
In me
In others
With respect

The same Words
Interpreted to sustain ill
These same Words
Construed and fortified
To battle
Against injustice

Parallels
Perhaps
But I need to learn
To sit within the midst of difference
And feel at home
I want to be empowered
To teach my children to digest examples
And to grow into character
Of images of good
Without distinctions
To recognize
The countless faces and facades of difference
Real and unreal
Yet understanding
Parallels

The path

Fascination and uncertainty
Adorn my recollections
of pre-dawn rambles along sugar cane paths
of stomach-churning rides
on the flat bed of a fume-belching timeworn Bedford pick-up truck
to harvest warm milk from dew-bathed cows

Today, my eyes impatiently
Examine my mind
and trace thin sketches from memory
of mist-soaked morning suns
Rising up quietly massaging the air
on my face
Before seeping into the skin of my clothes
And I ask myself whether
You would approve of the path
Life is choosing for me

My eyes copy the outlines of thoughts
Excavated
Transformed by nostalgia
Rummage through my mind
Like hunger
Ploughing ruminations for opportunities
to savor melodies of chortling egrets
Devouring parasites soaked cattle

I am forced to squint
To make shapes into forms of focus
To stop the vague careening images
From disappearing
I try to nudge my senses
To keep them sharp enough
to touch that life . . .
Instead
they quiver mindlessly
In response to police and ambulance sirens,
screaming clocks, door alarms
Insensitive smart phones and gadgetry

My eyes are no longer seduced
By the beauty of sunrise, the puberty of flowers
The simply react to images of crime,
Of corruption,
Of human tragedies;
of trite feel-good stories,
Platitudes packaged as news

I caught them staring at me devour breakfast in seconds
My attention focused on tele and a clock
And they too wonder how my tongue learned so quickly
To yearn for vulgar dishes,
Sodium-inflamed and sugar-infested foods
Leveraged on brightly lit supermarkets shelves
No longer interested in sun-drenched fruits
And vegetables sprinkled with oxygen
I hope you would approve of the path
life is choosing for me.

I think of the rapid response you summoned to my discomforts
As a child
The security you showered down to keep me safe;
And I ask whether
you would approve of the path
Life is choosing for me

Would you welcome the contemporary conveniences that surround me?
Would you scold me for no longer falling asleep to echoes of wailing
dogs teased nightly by fretful crickets?
Would you chastise me for not waking up slowly to adventurous roosters
arousing nervous hens and donkeys?
Would you reprimand me for forgetting so much?

As the sun rises over the grey distant mountains of my mind
I still wonder if you would approve of the path
Life has chosen for me.

My children

One races across the room and captures my attention
One pulls at my trousers and murmurs the word 'dada'
The other says "daddy it is playtime"

One child sings me melodies of smiles
One belches tantrums in choruses of discomfort
The other barters silence for long hugs

One speaks English and Thai, sometimes together
One gurgles in coos of laughter
The other asks me to read bedtime stories

One sleeps through the night
One cries and falls asleep in my arms
The other consumes me within her soulful eyes

These lovely creatures
Different in their similarities
Alike in their differences
Incompatible in their individuality, yet like-minded
And identical in my heart

Each gives me more reasons every day
To dream a life more memorable than yesterday's
To believe in possibilities reimagined
And to live
And to love in unforgettable ways

Always and forever

I would lie sleepless in the dark
Reflecting on the troubles that cloud my path
Longing for days without nights
Fighting hopelessness simply to survive
To stay alive
Then you found me
Dusted me off and reminded me anew

Always and forever
My love will stand by you
No matter what comes between us
My love will see you through
Always and forever

It was tough to believe
Unable to conceive
That my life could be seen in a different light
But now tomorrows come easy and success rests in my sights
The roads ahead no longer seem like mountains to climb
Just victories waiting for me to find

Cause I know in my heart
That always and forever
Your love will stand by me
And no matter the distances and troubles in my way
Your love is here to stay
Always and forever

I can't believe the joys now filling my life
The eagerness to embrace the nights
And the secrets—hidden in plain sight
I discover with delight
Because of you

And so always
Always and forever
Our love will stay brand new
And always and forever
I will be here for you
Always
Always and forever

You carry me

Each day your carry me further
Into life

You sculpt outlines of futures
On the shoulders
Of my heart
Challenging me to dare

Each day you carry me to new realms
On the gentle wings of friendship
Journeys made easy with laughter

You carry me with your smiles
And hold me so high the clouds of doubt
Are kept away by resilient warriors of love

You carry me
Through valleys of uncertainties
And lay me to rest across grasslands
Teaming with new life

Your eyes carry me
high enough to ingest mountaintops and to dine in forbidden paradises
Quenching my soul

You carry me
Places dared explored only in dreams
And fill up empty spaces

Great men . . .

Do not die . . .
They diffuse into dazzling constellations
Of light and stars

Great men
They live on through character and conviction
Their principles become defenses
Sealing them safely in our hearts

Great men
Live forever as monuments
To great deeds done without fanfares of vanity

Great men
Are the fortresses constructed by life to protect our memories
Like virtue reinforced pillars of our minds

Great men do not die
They go forth to prepare the path ahead
They build structures, roads, defenses
To shield us from ourselves
They sacrifice themselves
To teach us to understand
The present
Our blessings

Great men travel across boundaries of time and space
They float above the fray
Uninhabited by bitterness and guile
For their hearts sees the world as a family
Embracing all peoples

Great men do not die
They dwell in the shadows
They light our paths
And reign in our hearts

Walk into life

Come with me
Don't be afraid
Dare your eyes to embrace
New images of life

May I entice your thoughts to abandon tired memories
Affixed to the walls of your consciousness
And that perhaps, together
We could create just enough space
To hang small picture-glimpses of fresh possibilities

No rush!
Let's go slowly
To avoid repackaging the past

Give me your hand
And gently we take the first step into now . . . slowly
Without artificial stipulations
Limiting options

Easy does it!
No prescriptions! No advice!
No contrivance of daydreams
to fit within thin frames of exhausted pain

No rush!
Just let go slowly
Let yourself
Together with your mind take new photos
To decorate the chastened walls of your heart

Once you are ready
Take a picture
Any picture
Photos of your life
Alive
Without touch-ups
Just reflections of you
As you are
Now
Take this hand!
Only one baby step at a time . . .
with your eyes

Come on!
Look at me!
As we walk together
Through the thin mirrors of our eyes

Don't be afraid,
Take my hand,
We will sip life together slowly
—And in small doses—
Until confidence inebriates your senses

I ask
Only one simple step
to walk with me into the present . . .
Not perfect beings
Like those created in your mind
but as children of God
Imperfect and weak
But eager to learn life-lessons
and to grow into more complete souls
Together

The Master's Confessions

My dear subjects
Draw near
And bear witness
To my solemn declarations
Carved in stone on paper
And inked in wishful thinking

Hear ye
That these candid confessions
Are born of seeds once planted deep within me
And having gathered roots
They ruptured the fertile soil of my conscience
Hence I must speak

When she appeared before your Master
Emotions nude, earthy and brazen
Her face adorned with counterfeit demeanors
Her eyes smiles concealed the heart of demons
Beneath masks and charades
But
Let it not be said that your Master was duped
Or took leave of reason
For he stood firm in his fortress of restraint
And prevailed to this day before you

But it bears repeating
Lest there be doubt
The Master is not confused
The Master cannot be confused
Your Master is composed
Remarkable in his calculations
And steadfast in his rectitude
His feet sparkle in brilliant gold

Beware of the false-sayers
For they know not of what they speak
Know this and take heed
Though your Master hears their words
He heeds not the counsel of mortals
For he is wise—very wise

Winter's blast

Indifference blooms on stringy dried vines
Where white daffodils once smiled at cherry blossoms
And birds drift overhead on whispered voices

Cold stares
Now mix intermittently with wild whistled tunes
Exchanged briefly as tepid glances
On faces strewn across the streets,
Some float through parking lots,
In hallways,
On phones
Squeeze through narrow doors
Joined by endless hallways,
Opaque windows locked
With apathies

Some eyes
Skate swiftly by sheltered in thick clothing
Other drag people along on jagged cold winds
As fierce as paper daggers
Blown into the souls of strangers
Whose fortified indifference resists friendships

Today
A persistent sun corrupts the silence of hearts too young to hibernate
beneath winter's polished indifference
Suddenly
Lips begin to thaw
Speak to break silence
But say nothing

Persistent
The sun penetrates a High Street
In a rare sign of boldness
It challenges the still air
To reflect few tiny shards of the sunlight
To provoke a smiles
And force hearts fall on their swords
And once in a lifetime
A defiant sun connected lives lived separately
To reveal bulbs of emotions
Trapped beneath a heavy coma of
indifference

In his mind

In his mind
He always sees her not as she is
But as the little baby girl cooing in his arms
And his mind cries
For the woman she has become

In his mind
He tries to protect her innocence
And hopes that everyone does the same
He drives her to art class, and yoga and football
And his mind cries
When it realizes the woman she has become

He visits her on campus
He takes her for walks along the river
But frowns when eyes fixate on her
And wonders if their thoughts are pure
And his mind cries
Every time images of life forces him to see her
As the woman she has become

In his mind
He always dreaded the day
When he would have to tell life lessons, set curfews
Recast stories of yesterday
To hold off the inevitable tomorrow
And so his mind cries
When he remembers
The woman she has become

He walks her down the aisle
His arm clashed firmly
His soul convulsed in prayers
He hands her to the pastor
Not in panic
As the prisons of his mind released him

And this time his mind cries with the joy
At the woman she has become

. . .

Fall into naught

Memories are left in limbo
And night stays awake
By thoughts
Ripening into wishes,
But
Morning comes to quickly
And they all
Fall into naught

Days fly by
And nights become insanely brutal
As thoughts become ghosts
Stuck in rewind
Seeking, seeking . . .
Unrealized
Unable to take shape
The same conversations are repeated
And decisions
Are reopened and never quite mature
And again, they
Fall into naught

One smile

One smile
Fragrant
Delicious
Transformative
Lingering
For one brief moment

One smile
Its petals open wide
For its beauty to touch eternity
And provoked my eyelids shut
To capture within my eyes
The beauty
Of one smile
Framed
Protected on moist canvass
Captured in thought

One smile
Revealed
Its tenderness opening your face
And a new world

One smile . . .
One glimpse
One casual look
One frame
One lens
One permanent memory
Captured forever

Outlines . . .

A lone bird sang to a flower
Melodies
Quickly stolen by the wind
Anxious to protect secrets

The bird tiptoes
And kisses the flower
While performing enticing harmonies on restless wings

Again it kisses the flower gently
The flower is flattered
And bows slowly
Hiding her shyness
Without surrender

The bird floats away
Reluctantly
And the flower closed its arms
To shield itself
From the sudden downpour of gazing eyes

A lone bird returns
Sits a shy distance
On a fence
And whispers through its eyes
To a sealed flower
Would you care to dance?

The fence grew taller
The trees stood upright
The sun broke through the clouds
The lone bird retreats

The flower stretches into the skies
Throws open her arms
And blooms radiance

You Breathe

You breathed life
Into my lips
And stole
Sleep from my sight
That one night

You breathed life
And light into my path
Held me in your heart's arms
Cradled
Like a new-born
We spooned
That one day

You breathed creativity
It trickled down slowly
And
Seeped deep
Into my soul
It restructured me
Resurrected me
Delivered me
To me

You filled my pillows with expectations
Reveries
Delicately you stopped my breath
Brief
Only briefly

After I ingested every drop of you
Like morning dew
Evaporating in the misty sunlight
Sprinkled over
Breakfasts
Served fresh

Mount Nevis

Thick light clouds
Forever wrapped in cool air
Dance up and down
Uneven hillsides
Forming a gentle mountain
Enveloped in mirage
Yet real to the touch

Her beauty
Is protected within lush landscapes of distance
And watered by warm springs releasing in silent doses
Its torrential strengths
Its kindness
Meted out equally
To friends and strangers
Before
Turning purposefully cold
To hide its innocence from meddling eyes
Anxious to dissect
The mysterious delicate layers of Mount Nevis

Casual spectators
Beware
Of the camouflages of cloud cover
Shielding
Masking
The dazzling warmth
Preserved through the ages
From reach
And accessible only by commitment
Which pries open the gates
To this paradise
Guarded by hesitant hands shivering slightly
Over a heart brimming with compassion—briefly—
Then disappear again
As clouds roll in
Like heavy charging snow caps
To conceal the beauty of Mount Nevis

Tenderness

My dear old friend,
Have you lost your way?

Where is the almost tenderness
Once enjoyed in silent familiarity;
Where are the occasional hugs
The infrequent kisses, the cuddles
Frolicked in a handshake
And the warm conversations
Sprinkled into breakfast and dinner

My dear old friend
why the distance
Must you stand now in the shadows of yourself
Looking tired and even bored

Do you recall those endearing smiles you conspired
Over competitive games you lost
How about the cloak-and-dagger rendezvous
to inject warm spontaneity into the evening skies?

What has become of you, I wonder
Why now—the impatience
the weariness, the boredom

I see darkened heavy lines woven into your eyes
I hear the daily grind of responsibility
pull you towards the distance
to fill empty spaces

My dear old friend
What does your heart reflect today?
Can it even remember cherished moments
before fatigue claimed your creativity?

My old friend and pal, where have you gone,
I wonder

Don't want to

I don't want to want to
But I do
Want to
So badly that I want to
Tell you
How much I do

But
I have to pretend to
Not want to
Want to
Want you
When I really do so badly want you

But;
I dare not

I chastise my desires and tell them not to
Want to want
To be with you
Drenched in the rivers of your eyes

But I do so badly want
To reach out and say just how much
I want you

But I won't

Wishes

If this heart
Could talk
It would ask you to try

If this heart could hear
It would explain
The pain it carries on its shoulders

If this heart had space
To feel anything else
It would pray for forgiveness
To break free of emotions
Living eternally
Calcifying at the crossroads

If this heart could hope
It would wish wishes
And pretend
It is not too late
To turn nights
Into
Perfect day dreams

Lovers' Canvass

With his finger
He paints in tiny fine strokes
Secret images of corporal landscapes
Quietly
Depicting thoughts

He carves beauty
With his eyes
And reflects in bold sculptures
The dawns of golden sunsets

His strokes capture
Rolling breezes
Gliding along the soft peaks and valleys of her skin
And the moist warm smiles
Ebbing on her lips

His fingers mold dreams
Into realistic fantasies
Perfected
Light touches of twilight and rainbows
Strewn across
The calm panorama of her stomach

He holds the images up to the light
And wonders whether to hang it in the gallery of the world
As a monument
Safe from passers-by

But as dusk returns
He reconsiders
As his fingers retrace the nightscapes she designs

He decides to keep the canvass

Dear Heart

Don't fail me now.
You have gone the distance

Pay-off is not far away
Hold your ground
You can't fail me now.

Time after time
I have watched you
Jog mile after mile
Held your breath
During rough times
Done all the exercises
To prepare yourself

Heart, please don't fail me now.

Listen;
Brace yourself
Be bold
Stay strong
For just a little bit longer
Do not tire with nervousness
Do not succumb to temptation

And
Stomach;
You too, hold your ground
Reach deep down for those steely nerves
Stand firm
Shoulders back—erect
Ready

Here she come, heart

Please don't fail me now.

Poetry

Poetry . . .
Is the lens of the poet's soul
Weaved together by words and images
Captured on the tapestries of life

It tells stories' truths
Wishes wished
Thoughts hidden
Or expressed too openly
Of life lived vicariously

Poetry emboldens the reticent hand
To craft responses to emotions
Stories of life
Made raw by programed silence
It unearths and reveals
Sometimes crudely
And inopportune
But necessary

Poetry
Is sometimes mere words and phrases
Pre-packaged
To conceal sentiments
Thoughts ebbing and flowing amidst great fears
Rushing to be realized
Or to stay hidden
Not to be
Exposed to quickly and then
Discarded
Frowned upon with displeasure
And soon forgotten

Poetry
Is an escape, a quiet pretense
Sometimes, a premise
And sanctuary
Where wishes
Go to be reborn
Or simply die

Poetry is the verbal photography of life's moments that would routinely
Have gone unnoticed

Conversations with Pablo

Come
That I may imbibe the experience
And talk about the power of your pen
The insight of your words
Given life by poetry

When did you master the art to speak boldly
Of things I even dare not contemplate
Come, let's talk
About lips brimming with careful desire
About lust oozing
Untouched
Covered in nectar of delight

Let us imagine
Dawn spread across the Andes
Like soft blankets of snow trickled on open fields
Let's hear about bosoms blossoming
And thin black hair ruffled by touch
Fall to kiss the grass

Can we talk
About silhouettes of yearning
Innocence framed in beauty
Inciting cautious hands to boldness
To explore supine landscapes

Can you help me learn
To feast in forbidden gardens
On honey seeping from flowers
To reward my patience
Tell me Pablo,
Old friend,
Did you learn candor from experience
Or did it just leak from your pen

LOST

Today, his eyes
Became shipwrecked
Lost in doubt and
Regrets

They resented the past
And jealously despised the future

They became void
Emptied of emotions

And grew bloated with pain

Still they cried
And the whirlpool of tears
Carried him away
And he found himself trapped
Behind dams of despair

Today, they cried again
But they were silent tears
They had lost their voices

They grew incomplete
And soon formed lumps
Deep in his heart

Today, his eyes
Did not cry
They too
Became LOST

In my Father's eyes

In my father's eyes
I was a second chance
To rewrite future history
Expiate sins of omission
Committed mindlessly
In my father's eyes
I was an opportunity
To pass on lessons born of mistakes
And experience

In my father's eyes
It was possible to move mountains
To change the world
Recast the roles for which he was ill-prepared actors
And take on huge responsibilities
On the public stage of life

In my father's eyes
Our grandchildren would be architects of emerging empires
And fierce conquerors waging wars against injustices
Ensuring change from within
In my father's eyes
Life seemed richer
Materials were useless
Ego was contained
Friendship, compassion and family
Was true wealth

In my father's eyes
Mirrors constructed the future
Hindsight shouldered
Possibilities to renew

In my father's eyes
I see stubborn wisdom
Reaching out to teach me
Not to duplicate mistakes
Already lived in many fathers' eyes

One Kiss

She was convinced
One kiss
Would postpone the biting curiosity
And release her from the chains of never knowing
Whether she had chosen the destiny she knew
Or it had conned her

He believed completely
One kiss
Would suffice
To fill his longing
And knowing would quench his beleaguered appetite
And desire would be extinguished
Forever

They both soon realized
One kiss
Was all it took
To awaken desires
Neither one knew
Would be sealed in one kiss

And then

One kiss
Provoked another
And then another

In secret
They savored borrowed destinies
One kiss at a time
And awoke to realize
This safe risk
They could control intellectually
Defied the logic and chemistry of their lips

Half and Half

Love
should never jeopardize
Friendship

Friendship
should never endanger
Love

One
Must never deceive
The Other

.

They must
Coexist
Side by side
If necessary
Separate
If required
Conjoined within flexible distance
If this secures them both

But to date
There is no friendship
So clever
No Love so selfless
To carve out the required distinction
To live
Half and half

Lies

You ask me to pretend
Beauty no longer tempts me
Into long floating day dreams

You ask me to pretend
The taste of your skin tastes
Cannot sustain me

You ask me to pretend
Not to feel your smiles
Weighing heavy on my mind

But if I agree
It's all Lies

You want me to pretend
That the winds no longer whisper your name
In my face
And that the raindrops do not form
Misty images of you

You want me to pretend
That your kisses do not linger
On my heart

You want me to pretend
That pictures etched in my mind are just fleeting images
Of wishful thinking
Not the reality lived in my hands

You simply want me to pretend
But if I agree
It would be all Lies

Confetti in my eyes

The sun rose noisily this morning
Between
Soft pillows

The rains whistled slumber-like tones
On the quiet roof
Falling hard
To disrupt the images
Lingering on the morning air

Few trees cheered, sometimes loudly
Birds
Some lost in flights of fancy
Seduced by breezes of levity
Serenaded the sun

The wind clapped its hands
As the slow moving air
Created musical notes
That brushed over the grass
And pried the ground awake
To meet me

Then the sun peered into my window
Where my silhouette dozed gently

And again
A string of rain
Tapped on my window
To awaken my partner
To the surprise
Confetti in my eyes

KEVIN M ISAAC

Home at last

Curiosities drove
Insatiable feet
Stampeding
Into a quiet exodus to pursue knowledge
And collect bits of papers to feather nests

Over silent long journeys
Life stood watch
Encouraging forgetfulness
And offering reminiscences
To feel
The reviving fertile sun-swept Caribbean seas
Spectacular jagged peaks of the Andes
Wide embracing plains of North America,
Enigmatic seductive splendor of Asia
And a chance reckoning with a stubborn Europe

At long last
A nest seems to be taking shape
Erected high on stilts atop thin tall trees
Protected by low-hanging clouds
That cast aside memories
Of manufactured comforts
Excavated from unfamiliar feather pillows
Befriended inside foreign hotels

Finally,
The slumber of airplane engines
No longer lull sleep into these anxious feet
After long travel
As rewards
For almost
Coming home

Instead, the journey is enriched
By bounties of battles lost and won
Of thoughts marinated over easy recollections mixed
With dollops of mountain mist
That keeps teaching tired anxious feet
How to build a home
From a promise carved out of dewdrops on grass
And love murmured on the lobes of dawn
Picture perfect
Home at last

Tastes of Paradise

I gazed unknowingly
To the depth of her beauty
Her refreshed innocence
Her nude imperfections
And sough to discern the distractions
From the reality
But all seemed impenetrable

Her beauty grew cushioned in stern character
Canopied for its protection in hardened white clouds
Huddled together overhead in defense
Of a certain purity

Prostrate
Seemingly unprotected
Stretched out shyly amidst miles of desires
It satiated the taste buds of commoners
Who dared reach up to touch her blue strands in the distant light

I too hovered with the weight of obsession
Building in my eyes
To caress the probing warmth of the unknown
Savor the lushness of welcome
And differentiate beauty

I gasped for breath, for life
To live alive again
Without obligations
And regrets regularly
Soaking into the thin flesh of my conscience
Goading the stillness of heaven
To chastise me
And send me back to earth
Hopeful

I Wonder

When tantrums possess their arms and feet
And demons transform them
With fits of anger
Penetrating the air like bullets
Instead of words of reason
Or when they roll like fresh loaves on the floor
And ignore my commands
Scream hysterically in the stores and playgrounds
Forcing legions of eyes racing to scold and stare
I wonder
What this say of me as a father

When they turn up their noses at loved ones
And wave politely at strangers
Play hide and seek in public
And smile sweetly when someone
Pays them a compliment
I wonder what this says about me
As a father

When they tattletale and fight for my attention
Insist that I carry them at the same time
Feed them at the same time
Play different games with them at the same time
Bathe and dress them at the same time
Brush their teeth at the same time
I wonder
what this says about me as a father

Lessons in life

I watch them play together
Hug and stampede through the flat
Pillows, duvets, sheets, toys
Collateral damage
The raid the fridge together and plot strategies to win me over
Then I watch them scream
Hand gestures, tears, tantrums, stomping feet followed by shouts and fists
To mark their territory

I watch them, chase after them, hold them, play with them
Referee their fights
To help them learn life

I throw casual glimpses into their worlds
Today and wonder how different it would be tomorrow
Listen to their needs cried out over cocktails of tantrums and smiles
Scratches and Bites
Pouts and screams
Hugs lavished on me alongside and pleas for hugs
Which teach me a little bit more about myself each day

I swallow deeply thoughts that these are new beings
Different in every way
Similar
Different in alikeness
Yet reflections of the Images of God
Recollections of their grandfathers
Younger shards of me and their mother
Anxious to make their way—fiercely independent
Though gently dependent on the mosaic which is our life
It is not easy
And perhaps it should never be
This beautiful task of making this a to life
It is a lifelong commitment
Then I realize my new purpose

Blessed

They shout hugs without words
And thank me with smiles
They block the door with kisses in the mornings
And roll it back to embrace me in the evening

They say
"I love you"
With relish and sweet abandon
Investigate
Scrutinize
My every move
My every moment
And
Strip me of privacy
Cultivated judiciously
Jealously carved out over the years

They open sealed arteries
To my heart
And fill my head's empty spaces
With sweet conversations—some incoherent-
Concocted from new words,
Fortified with unfamiliar phrases
Gestures
And textures of sounds
Fed through inventive minds

I think of them
I feel their presence
Embrace their laughter
And crave their company
When sleep steals their musings

In the hurried silence
Of an office
Reflections shower me with remembrances
And I thank God
I am blessed

Apologies

His Heart
Does not mean to be intrusive
Indiscreet
And boldly
It prefers not to articulate what he entertains
In secret
But every now and then
Desire betrays discretion
And silence is numb from want

His Heart
Does not mean to say things
Which are understood
Nor make this world party
To his secrets
But time to time
Desire bullies patience
And hope grows dull from want

His Heart
Does not mean to be insensitive
Blundering
And childish
But time to time
Desire voids reason
And judgment drowns from want

His Heart
Does not mean to appear immature
Impulsive
And inconsiderate
But time to time
Desire trumps carefulness
And constraint surrenders to want

Ode to Poetry

Talk to me
When your heart needs poetry
And mine will write you verses
In proses and ballads

Talk to me
When your ears longs for a melody
And my voice's pen
Will sculpt you love-songs

Talk to me
When your mind whispers thoughts of me
And you wonder discreetly
And mine will build you Taj Mahals
To eternity

Talk to me
When your nights conjure images that daybreak
Pushes away
Talk to me
When you dream on me
And awaken to complications of language

Talk to me
When you speak to me
Without sharing thoughts
When absences invite remembrances briefly
And curiosity shines then quickly dims

Talk to me
I am always ready to listening

If hearts could talk

If hearts could talk
Mine would recite sonnets
Of love songs
Odes of poetry and verse

If hearts could talk
Mine would whisper melodies out load

If hearts could feel
Mine would be too sensitive to the touch
Share signs of hardening scars
Which sealed it long ago
Emptying it of old pain

If hearts could care
Mine would have been branded a hospice
Encumbered with the stories of strangers
And burdened with legacies of longing
And loss

If hearts could pretend
Mine would be a thespian
Of a thousand screens
A fort Knox of secrets
Experienced in concealing truth
The mind
Shuttered and discarded
A long time ago

Time

The years pass quickly
And even memory begins to forget
Where things are
Or how to draw out silhouettes of the beautiful experiences
Packaged and stored away permanently
In tiny strands of thoughts seared into me

I sit alone
Sometimes
To catch intimate glimpses
Of me
Of them
And of us
But Today
Beneath a light morning drizzle
I feel terrified
A little
As water trickles slowly through my mind
Washing away treasured recollections
Bit by bit

I am alarmed
Just watching powerlessly
My mind stares at memories
Of time-worn pictures still affixed to the walls
As monuments to a past

They share glimpses
Into thin cinders of your eyes smiling
Tucked away in boxes on the top closet shelves
They hold up the grace of your words
Sealed in layers in picture frames on the piano
They remind me of thick wallets of your embrace
Slipped deeply into my breast pocket
For safe keeping

But time moves too fast

Empty spaces
Are filled up by anxious ghosts
Who themselves
Appear haunted by neglect
They pace hallways
In my mind
Looking for company from a time long gone
They linger
To watch
Fireworks of memories
Ricochet
Through the ceiling
Fizzle
And fall into a secret place

Time passes too quickly
For me to see you through the rain
To touch you
Feel you
Present—close enough to remember
More than only reflections
Of times long passed

Time keeps passing
The drizzle stops
Yet the muggy dampness of longing lingers
Beneath hazy cloud-crusted London suns

In the silence
I venture a cavalier thought of a future
Transporting me back to the past
When time moved at a slower pace
When memories stayed longer
Not as mere reflections
But
Mirrors through time

Ruminations

Special moments
Morph into questions
They meander
And gyrate
Piercing the darkened realms
Of distant constellations

Unexpected
A formed shadow emerged from the bareness
Without answers
To disturb balance

The universe is unsettled
Brilliant thoughts rise
But
Jettison their belongings
Immediately
And all are trapped like tired stars
In black holes

Everything keeps changing
Dreams escape
Life numbs to the elements
And cherished thoughts
Become transient moments
Lost in a space

What is going on?
Who are these people?
Whose are these images?
Have they been lost or abandoned
Do they share a bond or a common destiny?
Can anyone feed my curiosity's hunger
With answers
And take away this hallow veneer
Where once stood
My life

Enemy within

Stealth
Cloak and daggers
Sinister foreign accomplices
Plot
Conspire
To propagandize
Disguise reality with misinformation
Campaigns waged with microscopic accuracy
Quietly in the shadows

Targets identified
The first line of attack is determined
The war is executed with precision
Bulls-eye
At Lightning speed
The taste victory savours falling below radar
To decimate all life in its path
Collateral damage
Dissecting skin
Devouring flesh
Emaciating bones
Eroding each tissue of resolve
And drying up every nerve of patience

Possible and imminent defeat
Summons anger
Suspends disbelief
Reinforces denial
And sends fear galloping through the weak epidermis of the mind
Where hope feels shattered
Fearful boldness tries to harnesses strength from uncertainty
Flowing into gushing rivers of emotions
Spawned within

The soul vacates the body briefly
Spirituality is clasped with grief to nurse comfort
Fear emasculates words of their power
Family draw closer
Science is tested
Prayers are shepherded to cast miracles
To transport
To transform
And transcend
To reclaim one more chance
And even out the odds
In stealth
Against the enemy within

Who continues to marshal conventional forces
And rally the troops into
An a formidable force
There could be casualties;
Pain!
Lots of pain . . .

There will be repercussion
Scars
Loss
Disintegration
Dissolution
Disbelief
Fractures
Fear
The scars of battle
Possible rebirth
Second chances

To fight on

Breakfast at Dawn

Responsibility
Exorcised zombies from his eyes
And duty woke him at mornings
Long before roosters tormented the village
And tickled the sun

His steadfast footsteps cleared away the whitish grey of morning
To let light through the windows
And tiptoed loudly across the wooden floor
To prepare breakfast and lunch

I still can remember the sounds of his footprints
Being engraved into the darkness outside
And mixing gently
With the cold dampness of dawn
Which awakened the dogs
Like magic

In the stillness
I could hear tails wagging
And the scent of their eager mingled with the food
Cooked carefully the night before over white-hot coals
I recall the agitated tap-dance of the chickens, rabbits and ducks
Assertive in welcoming a new day

We expected him,
Monitored his movements
And always feigned sound sleep
Yet half-asleep
Half-dreaming
Half-prepared
Half-conscious
Half-willing
Half-resentful
Our reluctant feet marched downstairs
Heaving lifeless bodies into a pickup truck
Where impatient dogs filled by pre-dawn excitement
Wagged welcome
As this mechanical beast belched slothful coughs into the air
And moved decisively
As headlights pierced the mist-filled road
Directing cold morning breezes over its shoulders
To strike our faces awake
And percolate into our clothes

Half-asleep
half-awake barely;
We nourished more dogs defending the night
Nudged vegetables from the soil
And avariciously
Drained courteous cows of fresh milk to feed villages

Encumbered by fresh bounties
The return trek forced our eyes into squints
Shut
But with enough room left to taste brilliant shards of light bleeding into
the air
Slowly
Effortlessly
We would clear away mist and dew with industrious steps
and pried open the sky with pep-talks
That chased clouds away to let in the shy sun
peeking over Dale Mountain

We marked our names with razor-sharp wet long grass
Ravenously kissed fresh breezes
And inhaled dew droplets
while sipping on sun-caressed milk
Sweetened with birds songs
Draining onto our faces from the buckets aloft
We feasted on festivals of fruits lining our path
Sneaked flavors into our pockets to reprimand hunger
As we walked
Having Breakfast at dawn

Mother

Her mild-mannered hands
Could sculpt dreams from marble-hard slabs of misery
And though
Alone
Lonely
her voice never complained.

It never surrendered to the frequent disappointments,
The missed schedules to collect his sons for a weekend;
To take him to play or for a ride;
Even to buy their forgiveness

She never spoke ill of that man

Instead
She learned to forget
The uncaring coldness of courtrooms
Furnished with callous tongues eager for gossip
Instead,
She worried more about unsympathetic lawyers
Indignant social workers
And impatient judges
Alienated by their indifference

She feared succumbing to denial
To the self-defeating arrogance of the shame
The tyranny of self-doubt
And the weight of abandonment

She decided to manufacture smiles
For her son, for herself, for his other siblings
she chose to subdue anxious birthday
With courage
And instead
She conjured up something from nothing
Wrapped gifts with songs
And rallied Christmas to become an occasion
For creative solutions

She learned how to dole out giant slices of cake
Baked fresh with old familiar stories of laughter and bitterness,
Frosting layers flavoured with painful longings,
Endless absences and lies
Mitigated by wise words and gospel songs

She knew well
How to harness the power of dreams
And to tether miracles
Snatched from the stampeding chronicles of life
To reality

And though they went hungry
She always fed them well oodles of dreams sandwiched
With stories of how the David of education
Defeated Goliaths of poverty
She taught them
To build new futures with fresh dreams
Not a duplication of her past

And as she beamed good-bye
With a twinkle and a breath
She filled their pockets full of lessons picked from life
And begged
"Use them at the right time
and build a new destiny"

Daddy did you hear me?

Daddy,
Did you hear me
Dance on stage last night

Daddy did you see the applause
Was it as long as you wanted it to be
Was it real
Or mists of my excitement
Daddy did you see enjoy the moment

Daddy could you hear the attention
Was I respectful,
And did I stand tall before the chorus of eyes
Shouting me praise to shore up my confidence
Was I poise and thoughtful?
I tried to deliver with self-confidence
While listening for your voice
to speak my name

Where were you, daddy
Did you find your prominent place
Highlighted in bold letters?
"Reserved"!
What did you think?

Daddy, did you see me
speak my mind to tease innate wisdom
the way you taught me
I looked for you all night
Daddy,
Why didn't you join me on stage?
Last night was our night.
Your night
We practiced for it for so long

Was it your hand I felt holding me upright,
Pressing gently against my back
To make my legs focus?

Was it you Daddy,
Standing in the back of the room waving goodbye
Just when I wanted last dance?

Take me Home

The green fields bowed their faces
Chilled by winter's mist
Spread like feathery blankets of air
Shepherding horses bold to brave the cold
They too, heads bowed
Eyes towards the water-lined ponds
Reaching up to greet them, defenseless
Quiet
Stealing my reflection for company

Then suddenly
Warm thoughts flood in
Rewinding me
Reminding me of sunshine
Punctuated by light rains and refreshingly blue skies
Hanging down to taste the scents of parched pavement

Beneath the light dusting of snowflakes
I vaguely spot trees
Green with determination of spring's promise
They bow and to say hello
And to kiss the sides of trains
In the near distance
A solemn couple of fearless birds ventured into the white silence
Then vanished within the loud noises of a lonely tractor
Standing in the middle of a field

Then suddenly
Warm thoughts toy with my memory
Of fresh succulent breezes
The aroma of lush young mountain ranges rising up
To embrace the endless blue sky
I could recall the tiny pearls of white sand nesting between my toes
Hear the boisterous calls of fishermen's' horn
Challenging the bellows of brown pelican
Scrambling to share the daily catch

As the train rambles north through clotting whiteness
Silence erupts
Penetrated only briefly by its cavalier whistle
Anxious to rouse life
Cloistered behind sealed windows and doors
Of incurious sleeping houses

Then I realized
Suddenly
The fields welcomed the cold,
They earth cuddled itself in the dull mist

As the cacophony of voices gives way to sleep
And inside the train
Suddenly
Images sprinted through the glass
Stirred and provoked my eyes
To the music of carnival winds
Transformed by the colors of a pale rainbow
The fragrance of kitchens sloping into the streets
Inviting strangers into familiar homes

The whiteness draws closer
To embrace the train
And an indeterminate voice speaks
"Ladies and gentlemen, were will shortly be arriving into Leeds . . ."
And
Another voice
Interrupts loudly
"Please take me home".

Stroll on the Thames

The sun finally
Rolled back the clouds
To reclaim its place
And an unusual blue patch emerged
Over London
Lingering
Lingering
The sun seared the glass wall
To pry me from the sofa

It scolded my children for their apathy
And before forcing them to rush for the door
It dished out lessons about health and exercised
And unplugged the tele

We discarded the sitting room hurriedly
And wondered
Whether to take
Coats and scooters
Or
Umbrellas and t-shirts

The boys darted into the hallway on scooters
With and keen daddy in tow and baby girl in hand
Chasing after them

KEVIN M ISAAC

Into the lift
We let ourselves become ingested
Though annoyed by the slow descent
Downstairs other eager neighbors
Had followed suit
Tempted to trust this virile sun
Under transition lenses I pointed one eye to the sunshine
And shared the other between my daughter
hunting shinny stones in the pavement
And two boys slicing a path into the distance on scooters

My arms reached down
To hold my daughter's smile
And my feet sought to retrieve faint silhouettes of my boys
Sculpted on the chilly air along the Thames
Just then; it started to rain.

Home

Despite the yearning bosom of the Coliseum
The quiet heights of the Spanish Steps
To the cheerful warmth of a Thai welcome
The rustling seduction of a Caribbean beach
This city beckons oddly
Its verdant parks relentlessly sprinkled by rain
Grey skies choked with clouds
Jealously rationing sunshine into small pockets
Hang low
Yet it beckons

It is not my home
Yet it is home
With its odd character
Welcoming me occasionally
Dismissive of me on occasions
Amidst an enduring eagerness
And affinity to embrace differences
Constant change
To dispatch armies of hazy charm like overzealous border agents
To greet me
With the genuine lukewarm handshake of a distant cousin
A Metropolis

Ambivalence in determination
To pull me in
But only close enough to boast of accomplishments
Sports, finance, tourism, hospitality, manufacturing, R&D,
security, of an aging former glory and conquest
Confident in contradictions
It tries to convince me of its enlightenment today
And its peculiar uniqueness in diversity and sameness

KEVIN M ISAAC

It is not my home
But it home to my evolving tastes
Imprinted on canopies of foreign foods
The brewing goulash of people, language, culture
And the admixture of multiple flavored desires
Rolled into one

It is not my home
But it is home to my children
It is the Realm
The odd sanctuary
To which they ask to return
Each time we leave
It is not my home
But it is a home
To extinguish their anguish
To teach them life
Acceptance
And contradictions

Candle-life

Bright
Yellow light
Red lights
Dancing softly to choral delights of night
Falling slowly,
Persistently enduring in songs
Reinvented along bands of late sunlight

Blue flames, green flames
Stretch beyond sight
Trapped in long tired yawns
Perhaps
Nodding to bow or simply take flight

White nights, bright lights
Slivers of shivers
Imperceptibly gentle
Poised in dignity
Postured upright
Throughout the night

It danced all night
Aloof, almost alone
Waxed poetic and untouched
Not even a blink
Flickered or flinched
As it danced
Mesmerizing twirls
And stretched to dazzling splits

Bright lights, late last nights
Candles burning, flames yearning
Hesitating, withering, tiring
Slowed
And extinguished
Before my eyes

The past

Like a discreet friendly magician
Spins tales of fictions
Into concocted miracles
Modernizes experience into enduring lessons
Teaches forgiveness
By draining hearts of atrophying venom
And allow souls broken by life's loads
To take courage
From second chances

It prompts smiles
To face down absurdities, uncertainties
to let you soar without harnesses
Through life's stormy winds
It takes you on fantastic journeys
With a mere slight of hands
Riveted in reminiscences
It captures and levitates your spirit
To reimagine dreams

It is timely and timeless
Its magic transcends ages
Secured like gems of memories in stained glass
Affixed in cathedrals of your mind

It reflects time
Transposes time
Recreates miracles out of memories
And lay them open
Across giant staircase of life

Art

A spark of light
Reaches out
In a cardinal embrace
It frames a figure of calm serenity
Cartooned in picture-perfect sceneries

Beneath supine slopes
Of possibilities
Undulating like soft grass kissed by winds
And nurtured effortlessly
By a ten-pack xylophone of colors
Like single-minded keys aligned
Woven delicately into hips
Moving smoothly
Slowly
To fusions of Mozart Symphonies
And tender calypso rhythms
Seeping from her skin

The light climbed down
On a thin vine of rain
To touch her skin quietly
But was intoxicated by flavors
Deceptive
Mild to savor and
Gentle to kiss
But potent

Her frame flows peacefully
Naturally
Serene like a river
Destined to somewhere
It holds small signs of light
Formed into tiny pebbles
Created with creative license
To visualize spontaneity differently
On the canvass of her face
She radiates ballads
Fashioned with lyrics kissed
Into her smiling eyes
Which conspire with lips
To promise discretion

Little Princess

I inherit her arms when I push open the door

She cuddles me with smiles
And showers me with the melodious masterpieces
Of the concertos and folksongs of the word—daddy

She cries when I step away
And chases after me
Freeing me of all privacy
Then summons me with infectious
Winks of mischief
And chastises me lightly

She finds comfortable sleep in my arms
Sipping firmly on bottles of lullabies and cozy kisses
Hummed on chords of silence

I feel her heartbeat whisper breath to mine
And tell stories I love
And I am loathe to put her to bed

In the morning
Musical notes shout cascading shades of dada and daddy
Racing to greet me

And
Once more
I am captive
To my little princess

Trust me

Your lives
Will be infinitely better
You will have running water
We will put more food on your tables

Your children will have better jobs
And better access to free education

Your streets will be cleaner, safer and free from crime
You will have infinitely more money
In your pockets

We will pave more roads to and from your local villages
Build more community centers, schools and clinics

When you get sick
We will fix you
If you need to see a doctor
You will get as many as you like for free

You will finally be able to own your own homes
Control your destinies
Plan for the future
And create wealth for yourselves
Your children and your children's children

We are the choice
Your only choice
For a brighter tomorrow
For a secure tomorrow

We are the only ones with the vision
And a proper plan to lead you and take care of you
To give you a more prosperous future

Trust me!
Take my word!
I am a politician!

Father . . .

Father, give me strength
To walk in your shadow
And to welcome experience gifted to me
Lived not only through my mistakes
But born of others greater than me

Father, give me strength
To hold my head high
During my heart's lowest moments
Feed me with your words
And the deeds of others

Father, give me strength
To lift up those plotting my downfall
And to rise with them on my back
When their feet falter

Dear Father, give me strength
To remain sanguine in the face of injustice
But resolute to conquer it
Show me wisdom in the little things
And raise my eyes towards heavens
Even when the gravity of malice's burdens
Drag at my feet

Father, give me strength
And embolden my resolve
To wear myself proudly
And never dress silent arrogance
In borrowed robes

Hear me, oh Father
Steady my mind's gait
Grant my heart wings of eagles
And my mind the courage of lions
Light my path
And although I am impure
Imperfect and vain
Give me strength
To be more like you

But for the Grace of God

Barely fathered
Mothered fatherless
Rationed skimpy diets of life
Through tiny windows of light
We struggled to make ends meets
In a one room gingerbread house

Denials and oblivion
Twin covenants
Sealed my sacrifice
Foresaw me a callous fate
Yet today
They begrudge my passing spring

They do not see
The labyrinths of shallow holes burrowed in the back yard
The permanent make-shift shower
Appointed with plastic buckets and enamel jugs
Where insecure privacy was sandwiched
Between unstable rusty galvanize sheets

They do not recall the limitless nights
Darkened by itinerant moons
They forget electricity turning up its nose and by-passing our house
and the water which stopped at the gate
Unless heaved on heads of buckets
To nourish life
And bathe clothing that grew on vines

They will not remember
Scare dreams moulded in worry-hardened clay pots
Tired soups thickened with smells of stale meats preserved in rock salt
They do not recall old bread
Toughened by patience and rationed on tomorrows' fears
Always, never enough to extinguish
Boisterous hunger brimming on mouths
Dulled with emptiness

They did not see me
Barefooted, racing to school
In white shirts and khaki pants
whose tones merged by overuse
While I chased the compassion of any opportunity

They may not even remember
Their ridicule
Ample to fuel despair
Sufficient to summon failure and numb a future
They did not see me courting sleep
To form destiny in the cover of darkness
On a shared single bed
Teeming with wishes
To overcome hand-me-downs

How easily they forget!

All they see today
Is resentment they serve themselves hot
On the rich canvass of their bitterness
Not the poor soul
Better placed yet still struggling
To become a real father
Albeit
In a five bedroom house with en suite baths
Two car garage, running-water, electricity
Family vacations and five star living

I listen vaguely to their biting stares
And stare down their criticism of envy
Clasp my hands and forgive
For I know only too well
But for the Grace of God
There I go . . .

Medusa

I have run gauntlets of doubts
Saved myself from haunted armies of wooden soldiers
Railing against me
I have protected my impulses amidst ancient treasures
And fought raging battles
Against cavalries of letters
Large letters
Ravenous small capital letters
Conspired with militias of words
Crusading with swords of shields
On mountainous battlefields

I have wandered through gauntlets of ambiguity
Found myself imprisoned by big words
Incomprehensible legions of words
Fed to me from poisoned chalices
Distilled with promises
Sequined promises
Dressed in lies to hide truths
About broken promises
Still-born promises
Given birth to mask
Camouflaged emotions proceeding in military-like precision
But I survived
By drinking succor from the cryptic eyes of Medusa

I have run gauntlets of deception
Muted by venomous charm
Unleashed in serpentine doses on my gorgonesque heart
Rock-hardened by aged quest
For answers
To nourish impatient carnivorous longing
To escape feasts of lies
Preying on the modest flesh of confused naiveté
But I stayed alive
By drinking the poison from Medusa's eyes

Angel

I glimpsed you last night
Standing on thin threads of light
Hands clasped
Saying a prayer
For the world
Through trembling lips

I spotted you again this morning
Your shadow perched against twilight
Legs folded in lotus
Casting spells and prayers
For the world

Mesmerized
I let my soul levitate
To feast on daydreams and constellations
Raining throughout the universe

Tonight
I glimpsed you again
Walking away
A baby cushioned in your arms
And laughter grafted on your gaze
In search of a prayer
To save your soul

Freedom song

Poverty
Unemployment
Bail-outs and leverage buy-outs
Bonuses and Lay-offs
Divisions
Decisions
Corruption
Poor governance practices and inadequate services
Poverty
Nepotism, Cronyism
Struggles discernible in years
Find optimism chilled under winters of powerlessness
Where to turn?

Wealth
Failing health, insurance cover
Pre-existing conditions
Tax hikes and economies on decline
Anxious to fill power vacuums
Demonstrations
Recriminations, rejections
Conscientious objections
Destruction
Violence and rebirth twinned
To let strength grow on vines
To feed life to nourish hope withering in darkened corridors
In dimly lit homes
Between bed sheets and thick pages
Beneath pots and pans
Shunning daylight

Poverty
Perennial in resistance
Resurrected, reincarnated
To watch wealth rise on the spines of poverty
Poverty emboldened
Enriched and ready to cast nest of blames
And to take blame
Against backdrops of fresh leafy trees decorating the river banks
Breast-feeding young fortune spreading in sheltered spaces
To protect new lives sprouting
Below
Way beneath
Poverty lines

Freedom!
Freedom!
Does it grow on trees?
Is it accessible to mortal humanity?
Can it be clothed in tangible messages?

Freedom where have you gone?
Do you ever grow tired of saving people?
Can your wisdom really transcend continents, cultures, class and
status quo?

Will you navigate oceans to build character on the hearts of non-believers?
Can you teach the oppressed faith in you to release them
That their faceless faces have a face in your voice
That their weaknesses are not permanent?

Can you convince them?
Poverty will not endure
But freedom will empower them
Eventually
To believe

Forgotten

Earlier
Three lovely enterprising girls
Rested on the retina of my eyes
But did not speak
Their innocence wrapped in tired rags
And hoisted on barefoot
Cart buckets of water
Too weighty for children

A sad laughter
Attended their lips
And their sleep-disadvantaged faces
Coated with shyness
Waved hello

Their muted conversation dried up
Beneath the thunderous arrival of bellicose loudspeakers
Announcing fresh campaigns
Slogans and promises

The girls walked on
And silence briefly recaptured the village
Before feisty little boys
Invaded my eyes
With playful shouts, fights, laughter, coughs
Darting from street to house and house to fields

KEVIN M ISAAC

Loudspeakers
Reemerged to announce elections
Calls for support and fresh mandates
As children continue to cart water bare feet
Schools pass them by on the sidewalks
Shrugging their doors with indifference

Inadvertently, I blinked
And they fell hard from my eyes

On the edge

Two shadows
Swathed in a light evening breeze
Danced
To the edge of dusk
Camouflaged by a hesitant fog
They sat next to me
Then asked my name

One shadow
Extended a hand
To initiate friendship
But demurred
The other shadow
Tiptoed back
Onto the edge of dusk
And invited me to dance
Then asked my name

My thoughts
Ambled on
Defenseless and willing
As two shadows
Massaged my weary soul
Beyond the bosom of twilight
I felt warmth
A deep breath
Covering my face
With delight
And two shadows danced with me that night
And both asked my name

Night lights

Sandwiched
Between colorful streams of night
Lights waltz in ecstasy
Where soft sounds meet silence
And deep sleep reveals clarities

I see clearly
Your face
Gently cradled by a flower
Resting on my pillow
Images appear slowly
And disappear quietly
Enveloped in night lights

In the excitement
Magic evolves like confetti
Life possesses my fingers
Forcing them to sing melodies
Of unspoken feelings
Conquered by night lights

Again your face
Taken by radiance
And framed by a jealous window
Surrounded in darkness
Reappears
Smiling as a Rose

My eyes cry

My eyes cry
But not for me

They cry for catharsis and redemption
They cry for the wary
They cry for hope defeated
And opportunities exiled

My eyes cry
Not for my heart
But for hearts deserted of innocent love
For love sown in desolate fields
Withering in the dryness of oblivion

They cry for souls
Emotionless and emptied by aloneness
Of life, busy mature children
They cry for caring love
Lost
In the presence of boredom
Screaming silence
While doors slam shut

My eyes cry
But they do not cry for me
They cry for pain
They cry for neglect
They cry to cleanse themselves of worn-out tears
To restore light to the rich soils of time
Hardening into rocks
Shaped by bitterness seeped within

These eyes cry
But they cry not for destiny doomed
They cry to turn hope's wastelands
Into oases organic green
They cry with a dream
They cry to be sure
They never have to cry again

And so it was

In the fall of life
As possibilities raced in on a cloud of wind
Sunlight dangled on branches
Leaves green with envy whistled
And other leaves colorful with delight
Jumped impatiently to the ground
In an orgy of wind, sleet, feet, rain and sun
That a flame took root
Fertilized with laughter
Smiles
Stories

And so it was
That new winds spiked with questions blew
Heavy
And machinations of the mind
Heaped under a cacophony of fears
Deluged within

Then flame flickered
Trembled
Nervously
Behind a long smile

And so it was that the fall of my life
Quickly froze over
Into a long endless winter

KEVIN M ISAAC

Silence

Rain scattered on windows
Wind tossed as bullets through locked doors
Floods
Storms back fire like cars
In silence

Feet hobble
Hands clap
Voices shelter from pouring rain
In silence

Engines gallop on damp pavement
Helicopters search for streets signs
Boats come ashore in shuttered houses
Silence

One man walks alone
His bravery outfitted in waterproof black jackets
Soaked to the skin
He journeys on still alone

Toddlers with white hair rail against the deluge drizzled
Into hands cupped as bucket umbrellas
Fall
To silence

Telephone rings
Voices comingle
Conversations contrast to the same end
Cold feet hobble to race up paved stairs
Dressed in soiled carpet marks

Windows awake
Dust themselves clean of deep sighs
Parked cars sit and float
In silence

Seething flower

She threw open her petals in a warm embrace
Her antlers and stigma reaching up to heaven
To drink sunshine and fresh air
In celebration of her coming-out day

This day
The transcendence of adolescence
Freedom from the braces that contained her
Shaped and determined her
Fell away old like petals

On this day
Immature outfits vanished
Her styles and filaments astride with poise
Stunning, dazzling and demure

She patted her sepals with youthful pride
As her stigma kissed the breezes softly
Unafraid, precious
Inaccessible, available
For all to observe and enjoy
From the distance

Fascination pushed him closer
He picked the flower
To admire up close
Alone
Away from predatory eyes

Locked away in his mind
She stood alone in a plastic vase
Dignified
Beautiful in radiance
She bowed her head
In anger
And withered

Hope

Whatever the occasion
She matched her outfits
With her expensive bare feet

She worked her fingers numb
To provide life
To build it as monuments
To all she wanted
And did not have
But promised to her children

She sculpted the future
In calloused hands full of dreams
And scattered them
For her children to reap

Undo everything

Un-love me that my heart never glimpses delight
Un-open tender moments mortared on my mind that thoughts never
revolve around you
Un-spoon me that my arms never relish the delights of nights
Un-hold me during sleep that I lie awake and alone without knowing
the joys of paired pillows
Un-kiss my lips that they are forever denied the nectars of harmony
burrowed deep into my sheets

Un-seduce me with flavored scents of your smiles that my eyes stay deaf
Un-speak words of love that I longed to hear that my words stay mute
Un-need me to never understand what being wanted means and to want
someone and have that someone want me

Un-dance with me long, slow, silly love songs that we never build an
anthem and my body never knows how to feel you
Un-whisper honeyed nothingness in my ears that intimacy never feels
familiar and right
Un-miss me that I never wander dazed in love, stand for hours in
airports awaiting delayed flights and longing
Un-encourage me to race home into your arms and crave the unhurried
caress of your hair

Un-remember me that I can forget memories we fashioned together
Un-touch me that my body becomes unfamiliar with the soft warmth of
your hands trekking across my skin
Un-enter my life so our path never crosses and my destiny feels complete
without you
Un-understand me that we have more arguments and recriminations
That my soul never feels secure with yours
Un-company me those dreary alone moments which became perfect
Let them suffer anxiety, distance and aloneness

Unsoften your heart that mine will always resent its coldness
Un-keep promises that disappointment becomes my reliable companion
Un-gift me the gentle melodies of your embrace
Unmask yourself that I stop wondering what could have been
And forget all that I want so desperately to forget.

For old time sake

When he broke her heart
She cried begging him to reconsider
For old times' sake
She sought forgiveness
She rummaged his eyes for one more chance
For old times' sake

She called mutual friends for help
Relied on parents and siblings for sustenance
And solicited compassion for her bleeding heart
For old times' sake
She promised to try harder
Become better and make him happier
She swore to forgive all his indiscretions
For old times' sake
She recapped the good times
Hand-delivered him special memories
To make whole a real future
For old times' sake

She reprimanded her family
Discarded chronic friendships
Quit work, stayed home to attend to him
For old times' sake

When he walked out
Pain consumed her strength
Nightmarish fear of the future devoured her voiding soul
And despair quietly conquered her heart
Before an unfamiliar courage discovered her
Cleared her mind
Reimagined his memories
And empowered her heart
For old times' sake

Hunger pains

These lips crave desperately the taste of well-seasoned
fried fish, curried conchs, whelks and lobster
The look everywhere for whole grain rice flavored with
pigeon peas, red beans and black eye peas
They pucker anxiously to reunite with some spicy black pudding
Fried plantains, baked sweet potatoes and creole chicken

They lament the nagging hunger for stewed "salt fish",
"salt fish" cakes, Johnny cakes, coconut dumplings,
breadfruit, dasheen, eddoes, goat water
They reflect fondly piping hot bread harvested daily from a brick oven
And flavored with yellow salty butter melting into the fleshy core

This nose aches also for the fresh air
Real fresh morning air chilled with a touch of mist
Rolling down the mountain to meet the sun
It still looks for a sunlit afternoon cleansed by persistent brief
drizzles which never manage to scatter a stubborn sun
It itches to gulp a firefly tinged night air cooled by
breezes skimming the sea as they clamor ashore
Then take their time strolling up to reach the village

These ears have grown deaf with the monotony of melancholy screeching
sounds of odd music, cars, planes and trains in to the windows
They miss being tickled by the rustle of trees seduced by light winds
And to dance with the energy of enthusiastic dogs, naughty cats,
Adventurous birds, restive crickets, panicky chickens, sheep, donkeys

KEVIN M ISAAC

This heart feels unsettled by nostalgia
Its taste buds salivate to kiss the fragrance
of a mango, a guava, sour sops,
To bite into a piece of sugar cane and feel the juices ooze
It longs for family to fill the void of a faceless city
It longs to play beneath a clean exuberant rain
It yearns for the predominance of nature
Affluent sunshine
Leading a carnival parade of sights, sounds, tastes and colors
Joined with masquerades, string bands, steel bands, brass bands
And real people

Bottle of dreams

Forgive me
I have not forsaken you
But hoped to find better luck
In a bottle

It warmed me
Provided friendship
An escape
From the world
Solace and sleep

Do forgive me
But when I called on your voice for guidance
You responded with silence
Always that annoying silence

At least
The bottle responded
It spoke clearly to me at nights
It granted me special powers
To control the world
To let it in or shut it out
My choice
Not theirs
Not yours
My choice
My world
My life and my thoughts
In a bottle

Do not forsake me, father
For I still need help
Maybe some blessings
And a miracle or two perhaps
Because the bottle was merely to tide me over
Until you could spare the time
To fill it with dreams

Whispers

Voices exchange ideas in conversations
About nothing
On everything
Send subtly subliminal messages to the head
To engage in conversation
When preference is to do nothing
They challenge
Scream energy into thoughts
And brandish ideas
Untested ideas that should vanish
But instead gain strength
And rise to the top of the mind
They take control and generate fears

These fears talk loudest
They are bold and irrepressible
They force the thoughts
To contradict their sanity
Question reasoning
And make the mind wonder
What is really real

Voices
Whisper thoughts unwelcome
Unnecessary
Familiar but alien and unbecoming
You become them
You battle them
Alienate them
Welcome them
And then become consume by them
Who are they?
What do they want?
Why do they haunt you?
Why do they not just go away and stay gone?

Voices
Messages
Thoughts
Contradictions
Evolution
Juxtaposition of master and apprentice
Control and ascendancy of thoughts versus fears
Explanations and confusion are coerced
And combine into a maze of voices and whispers that closes doors
To open exits
And everything becomes a circular game of voices and whispers

Patronage

Sponsor a child
For pennies on the dollar
Get a tax credit
Sponsor a child for less than a dollar a month
You improve his life
And get season tickets to heaven

Sponsor a child
In conflict-striven Africa
In disaster-prone Asia and South America
You will be giving her a real chance at life
Tell your friends
Invite them to become sponsors

Remember
For pennies on the dollar
You make a real difference in their lives
You buy them new clothes
Provide drinking water
And discuss it over afternoon tea

Sponsor a child far away
Anywhere but here
Far from the mirror
On the street corners weighed down with gangs
Unemployment lines dotted with school drop outs
Houses freezing without heating
People flooded from their homes
Poverty forcing some to go without basics

Sponsor a child there
But also spare some time for children here

KEVIN M ISAAC

Mind the gap . . .

Please
Stand clear of the doors:
Next stops
One Hyde Park
Egerton Crescent
Bishops Avenue
Regent Street
Via Oxford Circus and Edgware Road

Mind the gap
Please
Alight cautiously
Before monitored gates
Next stops
Kensington Palace Gardens
Hampstead
Chelsea Harbour
Grosvenor Square

Mind the gap
Please
Next train delayed
Fell free to summon
A textured Mercedes or contoured BMW
Buses to these locations temporarily suspended

Mind the gap
Please
Only delivery vans allowed to park on double red lines
To shop online in the doorway
Next carriage
Harrods
Ocado
Waitrose

Mind the gap
Please
This way, to private gardens
But no ball games and cycle riding allowed—
All dogs parked on leads
Or must sit on benches
Shaded by manicured trees
And watched over by police

Do mind the gap
Please . . .

He stood tall

He stood tall
Purposefully unyielding
Unpretentious
And rooted deeply
In sustainable soils of conviction

And although the world around him moved
He stayed focused
Even when the weights of his trials
Dragged him to the valleys of anguish
He coached his mind to build mountains of hope

When his body was battered and weakened
He drew strength walking for miles
Across the generous fields of his mind
And stood tall
Armed with integrity
His spiritual gait steadied devotion to justice
Pulled his feet free
One after the other
From the murky waters of persecution

He stood tall
Constructing confidence in all humanity
And held up his principles
As a raft to help others
Even when lies brimmed like rivers of violent force
Raged against him

He fought to ascend, to transcend
The pull of beleaguered flesh
Shrapnelled by faithful struggle
A warrior defiant
Even when age quiets his stance
He stood tall
One man above men
Not in height but
Stature

In the twilight

His years
Were saved in smiles
That held his eyes wide ajar
With contentment
Of a life void of regrets

His years knew peace
And restored his faith
Cleansed it and transposed it
To a serenely beautiful place

His years found enlightenment from others
And reaped joys distilled from companionship
Through the tenderness of grandchildren
The inharmonious songs of life's journey
Racing pass him
In its complex simplicities

His years found solace
In the melodies of the winds
The fluting sounds of water
The howl of animals
The hush of love
Whispered in his heart

And
In hindsight
He felt privileged
No regrets
And again
His eyes smiled
A gentle whisper which
Reached up to kiss my face
Before soon falling back to the bed

Tired . . .
They went to sleep

Still I wait

TO DENNIS

You stood
Beneath the thin cinders of dusk
Waved hello
Then
You were gone

I waited
Bewildered
Cradled by sorrow
Unable to wipe away tears
Flowing from my heart

They leaked pain
Into my soul
Which cried for your voice
Thrown from downstairs
Across the street
On the phone
Or through an early knock on the door

Still I wait . . .
And wait
Patiently to hear a familiar sound
A voice calling out my name

Still I wait . . .
For a gentle hand to wipe away tears
Firmly
And lead me back from the nightfall of goodbye

Still I wait
To see you again
To drown out the silence
Taking root in my heart

Still I wait
And weeping the loss
Race to shorten the distance
Dream to dull the sadness

Then suddenly
I see you one last time
Hands raised to your chest
One tear
Nesting on your eye

Now only silence remains
But still I wait . . .
And wait . . . .
And wait . . .
And wait . . .
And wait . . . .

In the clouds

Daddy . . .

I wish I could live in the clouds
And make my bed from cotton candied mists hanging the air
Fly about the sky on sun-dried cloud flakes
And eat long knotted raindrop noodles

Perhaps, I could race with birds
But only pretend, though daddy,
Since I do not have wings
I want to serenade the sky, softly
Watch people go by in planes
And dilute their noises with cloud cushions

Do you think I could use the breezes as wings?
And maybe travel the world with you
Dress up my eyes in white coats and sunglasses
To tame the sun
And stay awake

It would be fun to dream all day
And when I am tired
I could fall asleep standing on air
Not before washing my face in basins of waterlogged clouds
Then dry off with brisk winds

Daddy . . .
I wish I could live in the clouds
To keep heaven open
And an eye on world
From my cottony bed in the clouds

Inspired by Kaden

A city across the river

The unruffled air radiates charisma
Cryptic chimneys share secrets
Of mysteries seeping from cobbled streets
Who genuflect to fashionable boutiques
Supervised by wide walkways
Feasting on foreign dishes

Its narrow paved roads rise up
Speaking hundreds of languages
In one unique accent
Welcome joy sprinkled on unfamiliar faces
Schizophrenic with delight
Dressed in the stiff upper lip of pomp circumstance

It teases extraordinary dreams
To leap into the eyes of strangers
To catch glimpses
Of history's fantasies
Tattooed on museum walls

It cajoles you to stay over
To play, to indulge, to enjoy
Its surprises
Like valiant suns struggling to stay alive
Or to pierce impenetrable morning fogs
And hold off winter's menace
Hiding gently beneath daylight's surface
Cheered on by a daring rain
That will eventually disappear with graceful stealth

It embraces innovation packaged in relics
Laments discreet influence lost
And celebrates power reborn
In stock exchanges, technology and research
In global companies crossing the Thames on a handshake
To fraternize with high-rises
Towering with character

It smiles widely
Beneath clasped hands
And looks out over hurried feet
Driven to crisscross bridges
Navigate streets bantering with opportunities
Waiting at traffic lights
Or flirting with side streets
That race in cars caressed by shadows of buildings, busses, cyclist
In a queue

It breathes life
In tiny breaths
Tosses kisses onto parks
And swing open doors of more breaths
Into the heart of a city
Reborn
Each day

In the eyes of love

Staring into the eyes of love
Revealed no expectation
Colors
Faces
Races
Or genders

They were pure
Uncomplicated
Void of rancor
Prejudice and judgment

They stared right back at me
Innocently
And spoke the words
Compassion
Friendship
Understanding

Who you are

Maybe I should have told you
I love and respect you
As you are
Maybe I should have told you
We each find our path in life
As individuals

Maybe then
You would not have feared
Telling me your truth
Sharing the pain closeted with joy
Hidden deep inside
To protect from ignorance
And intolerance

And maybe I should have said
I am proud to be your father
And I love you
For who you are

Welcome to this moment

The smile of your eyes
Found forever in me
Even when it prefaces the inventive creativity of your hands
For mischief

Your laughter
Inscribes lasting memories on the eternity of my heart
And encourages my admiration
To treasure you even more

I look out at yesterdays
And aspire for tomorrows
But always
Find myself thankful
To welcome this moment

Serenades

Memories
The thin vapor paths to yesterday
Linger on my mind
Like warm songs
Touched softly on a grand piano
Fused in a ballad of sounds
Too precious to be voiced

They reach across time
Space and eternity
To build bridges to you
To hold you

As they evaporate slowly
With the ripening of the sun
And the twilighting of days
I still feel their aftertastes
Drifting
But soaking into the skin of my now
Like long classic serenades

Today

I hear the sounds
Of people eager to move ahead
To steal insights around the bend
Over the horizon

They don't feel the quietness of silence
Taste the sweet stillness of nothingness
Their hearts are not yet still
They crave the emergence of newness

And lose sight of the beauty before them
But
Let tomorrow take its time

I have today

Unanswered prayers

God must have heard
My infinite wounded pleas
Offered as payers
To design my life
In the image of my past

But
He must have ignored them
Ignored me
Chastised me with silent rebuke
Closed doors
To starve my eyes of desires
I thought best for me

Instead
He steered me along this winding path
To you
Pushed me forward
Even when my eyes
Camped on my shoulders
Could only look back
Hoping to chain my life to that familiar past

He persisted
In disnoticing my pleas
He pointed me
Ahead

When finally my resistance weakened
And withered
The future found me
Ready
And grateful
For unanswered prayers

What if

The world is an illusion
Camouflaged in realism

What if we woke up one day and learnt
That cures for chronic diseases are concealed
Because treating symptoms is more profitable

What if we discovered
That science and religion were bogus
Concocted
To tame human spontaneity

What if we found out
That all politicians lie
And keeping their jobs
Trumps doing the job

What if we woke up to realize
That the truths we know were false
And our teachers were unreliable

Would we do anything differently
Would any of this matter
Would we simply carry on
Heads masked in ignorance

Or would we start
The revolution

A vessel

Lord, please make me
A vessel for the world . . .
Lift me up in moments darkened by despair
When galloping anxieties plough
The unsettled oceans of my mind like reckless warriors
Transform me into a compass
And point me to dry lands

Dear Lord, steady my vessel with courage
To endure torrential waves of doubt
Keep me resolute in days greyed with pain
And on course like a beacon shining warmth
For the world

Lord, please steel me
Make me into that unflinching shoulder
Of support and comfort for those in need
Blind my mind, dear Lord, to bitterness
But open to the magnificence of the heart
Help me
Amidst the frailties and imperfections of this life
To love permanently without judgment
With compassion to all

Strengthen me
To resist my common vanity
To walk in my brothers shoes
And understand my sisters' voice
Let me always see them in me as me
And never abandon them
For their failures and successes are my own
I am their keeper

Dear Lord, I ask you
To make me a vessel
Build me from the metal of my children's hearts
And the innocence of their eyes
Teach me to forgive
To embrace kindness and truth
Fortify my heart, dear Lord
To be that vessel in your image
And your message
To be a candle for the world

On your own

We come alone
Though not quite
And
We depart alone
Essentially

But
Throughout the journey
We are never
Really
Quite alone

We are
Nurtured and nourished
Skilled and educated
Comforted and loved
Protected
Carried along
On many silent shoulders
Led into greener pastures
On the backs of strangers
Who let us feed on life
Dine on new and fresher experience

We feast on the wisdom of elders
And ingest the souls of companions

We come alone, partly
And we leave alone
But never really do we traverse life
Alone
We rely on the paths sown by other seasoned travelers
To lead us to the banquet halls of dreams
Where we feast and learn
Over Breakfast with our fathers

In God's hands

I hope the roads ahead stand up
To welcome your feet
And modesty accompanies your strides,
Always
And that love sustains your journey
To find peace in God's hand

I hope you never forfeit dreams to deceit
But when you do,
May God's hands chastise its many incarnations
And that you recognize the changing faces of ambition
Manufactured as vocations
Even when they dress themselves
In pretences as tender as silk

I hope you never feel compelled to yield character
To the anguish of defencelessness
Nor betray worthy pursuits
Out of fear your faith may not find
Humble sanctuary
In God's hands

I would welcome a miracle!
And like him,
I promise! I do listen! But, I can only listen!
For unlike them
Full of wisdom and ad-vice
I am not a God
Determined to re-cast lives and destinies—

I am but this battle-weary traveller
Without a name
Wandering trying roads in ignorance;
In search of wisdom
Often
Wondering whether the Gods
Mock my simplicity

Inside a lie

Ducking shadows
Chasing silhouettes
Painted partially on unripe dreams
Left to cocoon inside consummated memories
Protected by the humble silence
Of alienated words
Spoken to intimidate lips
Which communicate only rehearsed spontaneity
Walking side by side
With a truth masked behind creative stories
Living happily
Inside a lie

Lives mirror in parallel
Dissimilar only in minute details
Erect thin impervious walls
To seal the silence
Between friends,
Recollections and stories
All sanitized in Russian roulettes
Discharged as smiles,
Manufactured layers of realities
Decorated to thrive peacefully
Inside a lie

Better Angels

In giant kilns of his mind
Anger forges rigid thoughts into steel bars
Welded with relentless attention
It created impenetrable walls
Surrounded itself by moats
Filled with tiny spikes of retribution

In the reservoirs feeding his mind
Irritation simmered like leaven
And fermented frustration
Became trapped inside harsh words
Which isolated and entrapped him

In time
His mind's sanctuary withered
Discord reigned
Revenge's lust coerced him
And persuaded him to bide his time
That one day he might relish the flavors of vengeance
Served cold

In time
The preserve of his mind
Became populated with chaos
Deprived of restful sleep
Haunted by the hostility of inventive mischief
And in the end
Its serenity was violated,
Perverted
And lost
It was shepherded by others
Enslaved by their actions
Led by demons within

He awoke to learn
His mind had gained nothing
From shutting out the voices
Of better angels

Simple pleasures

Guiltless,
Gently
Falling . . .
Caught by my partner's eyes
I tread water on grass
Lounge aimlessly on the spines of sunrays
Drenched in perennial thoughts floating
Beyond my mind
Rendered blank by absorbing light
Walking across the park to greet my lips
Frolicking with ice-cream
While dodging birds and courting ducks

Falling
Slowly slowing
I drop softly into the embrace of natural aromas
Carved from long nights
Tasty take-away from fashionable restaurants
And tiptoeing tastes
Racing to steal small bites
Cheesecake
Chilled wine
Divine

Drifting
Through wild open countryside
Eating fresh air
Soaked with clean rain
Driving with windows down
Breezes tapping my face
Lifting my smiles up into those very few clouds
Stretched thin like cotton candy
To expose blue skies

Drifting
Through corn patches and mustard fields
I see distant smells like sheep
Cattle and horses populating the landscape like shrubs of green grass
I wave the wind forward
With my childish gaze
Before falling again

We take fresh walks along the river
Smile with children
On scooters and bikes
Uttering words
Just words
Bringing forth joys wrapped like sweetened fantasies
Covered in real laughter
Leaking from their eyes

About the Author

Kevin M Isaac is and senior diplomat and author of two previous collections, Whispers of Silence (1998) and Memories in Serenade (2010). He was born and grew up in the pristine Caribbean island of St. Kitts Nevis. He studied in the Caribbean, France and the United Kingdom. He has been writing for more than two decades and describes his poetry as oral photography of life. As a UK Chevening Scholar in 1994, his poem "Culture Shock - Rain over Birmingham" was awarded first prize for poetry by the Foreign and Commonwealth Office. He holds graduate degrees in international relations, diplomacy and international economic law. Since 2011, he has been residing in London, England where he serves as his government's High Commissioner (Ambassador) to the United Kingdom.